FIGHTING FORCES IN THE AIR

F/A-22 RAPTOR

LYNN STONE

Rourke
Publishing LLC
Vero Beach, Florida 32964

www.rourkepublishing.com

PHOTO CREDITS: All photos courtesy of the U.S. Air Force

Title page: *The sun sets on a Raptor at rest.*

Editor: Frank Sloan

Library of Congress Cataloging-in-Publication Data

Stone, Lynn M.
   F/A-22 Raptor / Lynn M. Stone.
      p. cm. -- (Fighting forces in the air)
   Includes bibliographical references and index.
   ISBN 1-59515-180-X (hardcover)
   1. F/A-22 (Jet fighter plane) I. Title. II. Series: Stone, Lynn M. Fighting forces in the air.
   UG1242.F5S782 2004
   623.74'64--dc22

                                    2004011743

Printed in the USA

CG/CG

TABLE OF CONTENTS

F/A-22 RAPTOR

The Raptor F/A-22 is the U. S. Air Force's first new fighter of the 21st century. The Raptor has been designed with state-of-the art **avionics**, high-tech weaponry, and **stealth** technology. The Raptor is expected to be a major improvement over the Air Force's highly regarded F-15E Strike Eagle fighter.

The new F/A-22 Raptor is a fighter with stealth technology, making it almost invisible on radar screens.

▲

A green HUD (Heads Up Display) for the pilot shows in the cockpit of a Raptor, the world's most advanced fighter aircraft.

The F/A-22—"F" for fighter and "A" for attack—borrowed the best qualities from earlier American fighters like the F-15E, F-117, and **multi-role** F-16. The Raptor's clear, bubble-top **canopy**, for example, is similar to the F-16's. At the same time, the F/A-22 was designed to take advantage of recent advances in materials, avionics, **airframe** design, and engine performance. The result is an aircraft that has "first look, first shot, first kill" capability. In short, the Raptor should be able to find, fire at, and destroy an enemy aircraft before the enemy plane can react.

F/A-22 Characteristics

Function: Multi-role fighter

Builders: Lockheed Martin and Boeing

Power Source: Two Pratt and Whitney F119-PW-100 turbofan engines with afterburners and two-dimensional thrust-vectoring nozzles

Thrust: 35,000-pound class per engine

Length: 62 feet, 1 inch (18.9 meters)

Height: 16 feet, 5 inches (5 meters)

Wingspan: 44 feet, 6 inches (13.6 meters)

Speed: approximately 1,500 miles per hour (2,400 kilometers per hour)

Ceiling: more than 60,000 feet (18,288 meters)

Maximum Takeoff Weight: classified (secret)

Range: classified (secret)

Crew: One

Date Deployed: 2005

The two-engine Raptor has **supersonic** speed at the **Mach** 2 level. And with its twin-fin tail and lightweight airframe design, it has outstanding **maneuverability**. But much of its ability to dominate sky warfare is rooted in its remarkable, on-board technology. It helps Raptor pilots fly, find, and target enemy aircraft and avoid enemy surface-to-air weapons. Overall, the electronic systems and computer support in a Raptor provide the pilot with features that will allow safe, efficient control of the skies. That air dominance, in turn, can help protect other American aircraft, as well as ground and naval forces, from air attack.

FACT FILE ★

"RAPTOR" IS A NAME GIVEN TO HAWKS, EAGLES, AND OTHER BIRDS OF PREY. THE RAPTOR GIVES THE AIR FORCE WHAT IT EXPECTS TO BE THE WORLD'S MOST **LETHAL** BIRD OF PREY.

FLYING THE FA/-22

The Raptor brings to the U.S. Air Force a faster and more maneuverable fighter than previous fighters. The F/A-22's two Pratt and Whitney engines provide a higher **thrust** to weight ratio than previous engines. In other words, the engines produce greater forward power— about 35,000 pounds of thrust each—in relation to the aircraft's weight. The F/A-22 also has a carefully designed shape.

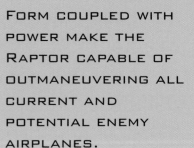

FACT FILE ★

FORM COUPLED WITH POWER MAKE THE RAPTOR CAPABLE OF OUTMANEUVERING ALL CURRENT AND POTENTIAL ENEMY AIRPLANES.

A Raptor roars over clouds above Edwards Air Force Base, California. ▶

▲ *The twin-tailed Raptor may be the world's most deadly "bird of prey."*

The Raptor's shape and the materials used in its airframe give it another advantage—stealth. Stealth aircraft, like America's B-2 bomber and F-117A Nighthawk fighter, may not always be invisible to enemy radar, but they are very difficult to observe on radar. Their low, smooth profiles are helpful in avoiding radar detection, but so, too, are the new airframe materials that deflect radar energy.

Radar sends powerful sound waves to find targets, but certain shapes and materials tend to bounce and scatter radar waves. A stealth aircraft may appear to be no more than a bird on a radar screen. Aircraft like the Raptor are said to have a small "radar signature." That makes them, of course, much tougher game for radar-tracking devices.

▲ *The Raptor's airframe is designed to leave a small radar signature.*

▲ *An airman uses a non-contact thermometer while curing the special coating on a Raptor airframe.*

The Raptor's lightweight and radar-deflecting airframe is a mixture of several materials. It has titanium, aluminum, steel, and blended materials, such as thermoplastic.

Nearly 40 percent of the airframe is titanium, used for its relatively light weight, strength, and heat-resistant properties.

A small radar signature is an important means of aircraft survival. But the Raptor also has survival built into its engines. The Raptor can roar along at supersonic speeds without using its **afterburners**. (It does have afterburners for emergencies.)

▲ *A Pratt and Whitney F-119 engine runs in full afterburner mode during a test at Tyndall Air Force Base, Florida.*

Flying at supersonic speeds, the Raptor can enter an efficient "supercruise" mode. A Raptor will normally fly at a **subsonic** speed—a speed less than the speed of sound. But the airplane can also fly at Mach 2, twice the speed of sound, or about 1,200 miles per hour (1,920 km/h) near sea level. At higher altitudes, where Raptors normally fly, the air is thinner than at sea level. The speed of sound—and airplanes— increases because sound waves meet less resistance in the lighter air.

▲

Despite having two powerful engines, the Raptor is a relatively lightweight aircraft.

Avionics are the electronic systems that help a pilot fly. Among other things, F/A-22 avionics include a central "brain" with powerful computers and high-quality, high-tech cockpit displays. Raptor avionics allow the pilot to concentrate on the plane's mission rather than on managing individual sensors.

The integrated avionics system of a Raptor is known as Block 3.0 software. This system provides the Raptor's "first look, first shot, first kill" capability. Block 3.0 has the electronics and multi-sensors that allow the Raptor to locate, follow, identify, engage, and finally destroy several targets.

▲

At higher altitudes, where air is thinner, a Raptor can fly faster and burn less fuel.

CHAPTER THREE

Ground crews fit a Raptor with weapons for a particular mission. The weapons it carries for one **sortie** may not be the weapons it carries on the next.

The F/A-22 carries much of its firepower in three internal weapons bays. It can pack six radar-guided AIM-120C medium-range air-to-air guided missiles (AMRAAMs) in the main weapons bay. Each side weapons bay holds a short-range, heat-seeking AIM-9M Sidewinder missile for air-to-air combat. Sidewinders are well named because they twist and turn like a sidewinder rattlesnake.

▲

In a high-speed test flight, a Raptor fires its afterburners.

The Raptor also has an advanced M61A2 Vulcan 20mm Gatling gun above the right air intake. The gun has six rotating barrels, so none becomes overheated during rapid fire.

For air-to-ground attack, the Raptor can carry two 1,000-pound class (455-kg) joint direct attack munitions (JDAMs) in place of four AIM missiles.

▲

A Raptor pilot is surrounded by high-tech electronics in the cockpit.

JDAMs are "smart" bombs. Equipped with computers and satellite navigation systems, they can fly themselves into a selected target.

Carrying weapons internally helps the Raptor keep its stealthy profile. The F/A-22 can, however, be fitted with additional weapons or fuel tanks at four stations on the outside of its airframe.

▲

F/A-22 pilots learn about the Raptor's weapons and weapon controls on a flight simulator.

COMING OF AGE

The F/A-22 is a product of more than 20 years of thought, research, and development. As early as the 1970s, the U.S. Air Force realized that it would need a new-generation fighter to replace the F-15 Eagle and the F-15E Strike Eagle that followed.

▲ *A Raptor fires an AIM-9 Sidewinder missile from its side weapons bay.*

▲ *A Raptor shows its side weapons bays as it rolls into a turn.*

The Air Force was particularly worried about new fighter aircraft being developed by the former Soviet Union, a potential American enemy. But it was also concerned about new surface-to-air missiles that might down an F-15.

In 1985 the Air Force began a program that sought a new, dominant fighter. The airplane would use new, lightweight building materials, have advanced flight control systems, more power, and stealth capability. The first models of the new plane were ready in the late 1980s.

▲

The Raptor (background) is gradually replacing the U.S. Air Force's F-15 Eagles (foreground in photo).

Tests and modifications of the F/A-22 continued into the 1990s. The first flight of a Raptor took place in September, 1997. The first Raptor was delivered to the Air Force's Air Combat Command in January, 2003, for more testing. Raptors first became operations-ready in 2005.

▲ *The world's first combat-ready stealth aircraft was the U.S. Air Force's F-117A Nighthawk.*

FLYING INTO THE FUTURE

Raptors will gradually be phased into Air Combat Command units to replace F-15s. Eventually Raptors will replace F-15Es. The Air Force plans to purchase 339 Raptors, but that number could change because of budget or political factors.

The Air Force expects to have nearly 80 F/A-22s combat-ready by 2008. Not long afterward, the Air Force also plans to have the first F-35 Joint Strike Fighters ready.

FACT FILE ★

THE JSFS ARE CONSIDERED TO BE MORE OF A SURFACE-ATTACK AIRCRAFT THAN THE F/A-22.

▲ Another new American combat plane, the Joint Strike Fighter (JSF), will begin service soon after Raptors become operational.

▲

Raptors will eventually replace America's F-15E Strike Eagles.

Advances in military aircraft continue in nations other than just the United States. There are several new, 21st-century jet fighters, including Russia's SU-35. But of particular concern to the U.S. Air Force is the export of jet technology to potential enemy states. Also of concern are improvements in antiaircraft and ground radar technology. Both put American warplanes—and American air superiority—at some risk. The Air Force, however, is convinced that the F/A-22 will continue to give it air superiority.

Raptors are scheduled to be built through 2013. The Raptor was designed to accommodate new avionics and weapons systems as they become available. Those modifications should keep the F/A-22 current well beyond 2013.

Glossary

afterburners (AF tur BER nurz) — devices for injecting fuel into a turbojet engine's hot exhaust gases and burning it for extra thrust and speed

airframe (AIR FRAYM) — the wings and shell, or body, of an airplane without its engines or weapons

avionics (AY vee ON iks) — the electronic systems and devices used in aviation

canopy (KAN uh pee) — the enclosure over a pilot and airplane cockpit

lethal (LEE thul) — deadly

Mach (MAWK) — a high speed expressed by a Mach number; Mach 1 is the speed of sound

maneuverability (muh NYUV uh ruh BIL uh tee) — the ability to make changes in direction and position for a specific purpose

multi-role (MUL tee ROLL) — capable of being used in more than one way

sortie (SORT ee) — one mission by one plane

stealth (STELTH) — the technology and various strategies used to make an aircraft invisible to radar detection

subsonic (sub SON ik) — any speed below the speed of sound

supersonic (SU per SON ik) — any speed above the speed of sound

thrust (THRUST) — the forward force of an object; the force produced by an aircraft engine

INDEX

FURTHER READING

Green, Gladys and Michael. *Air Superiority Fighters: F/A-22 Raptors.* Capstone, 2003
Sweetman, Bill. *F-22 Raptor*. Motorbooks, 1998
Sweetman, Bill. *Lockheed Stealth*. Motorbooks, 2001

WEBSITES TO VISIT

http://www.af.mil/lib/airpower
http://www.af.mil/factsheets

ABOUT THE AUTHOR

Lynn M. Stone is the author of more than 400 children's books. He is a talented natural history photographer as well. Lynn, a former teacher, travels worldwide to photograph wildlife in its natural habitat.